Learning to
Die /
Learning to
Live

Learning to Die / Learning to Live

Robert M. Herhold

FORTRESS PRESS
Philadelphia

Library of Congress Catalog Card Number 76-007861

ISBN 0-8006-1232-9

5766F76   Printed in U.S.A.   1-1232

To my parents and brothers

Learning to Die /
Learning to Live

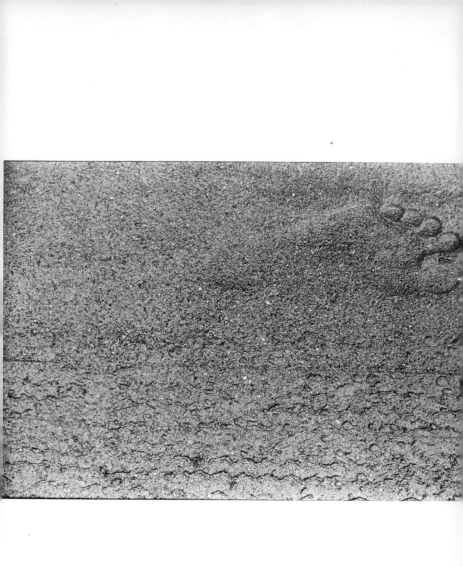

It is too bad that dying
    is the last thing we do,
Because it could teach us
    so much about living.

Rachel weeping for her children;
she refused to be consoled,
because they were no more.
———

A friend asked himself aloud: "What is it about death that I do not like?" For him it was the loneliness of placing a child in the ground.

I do not like the arbitrariness of death as it barges into our lives, often when we are least prepared. If life is meant to be a "growth in grace" then what grace is there in cutting someone down while that person is still growing? What justice or love is there in taking a father from his dependent children? Why should a young researcher be stricken with the very cancer she is seeking to cure?

It takes some of us longer than others to catch on to the purpose of life. I am just beginning to sort out my priorities and to discover my values, and already my life is two-thirds over. Now I fear that the game will be called because of darkness before I get my chance at bat.

I do not like the mystery surrounding death. To trade this bittersweet life for something totally unknown requires strong faith. Such faith exists independent of scientific support. Why does God put us to a test which strains even the strongest faith?

Most of all I dislike death for separating me from those who are nearest and dearest. It takes much painful growing to develop a good relationship with a husband or wife, only to have it end almost as soon as it begins. The bonds between parents and children, between brothers and sisters, between friends are too precious to be broken gracefully. The wrench, the stab, the endless years of loneliness produce more pain than humans should have to bear. I marvel when I see how people have lived with their losses.

I am not sure what holds people together when someone close dies. The thought of heaven is surely a comfort to some, but that does not cure their present loneliness. Some people try to lose themselves in work or in pleasure. Others question God's love, but somehow go on believing.

I can only fall back on the incredible notion that in Jesus, God is sharing the worst with us. Jesus is God's vulnerable side. In Jesus, God learned what it means to live and to die as a human being.

Anything less than this is inadequate to the awesome task of learning to die—and to live! ❧

Do not go gentle into that good night.

. . . .

Rage, rage against the dying of the light.

———

I do not want to hear about "sweet death" or "peace at last" or "eternal rest." I agree with Paul who called death "the last enemy." I heard a gentle person cuss when he talked about his brother's fatal heart attack. When an unusually close and caring marriage was ended by death, the wife said that she did not want to hear any of that "death and dying baloney."

That is honest. Those reactions could have more to commend them than a rack full of sympathy cards.

I think that anger is all right with God. Maybe a few angry words even escaped his lips as he watched men drag his Son to a garbage dump to be killed.

Anger is supposed to be one of the emotions we work through on the way to the final acceptance of death. That is OK for the dying person, but the rest of us still feel cheated since a big part of us dies when someone close is cut down and taken from us. Also, it reminds us of something we do not like to be reminded of—the rapidly approaching end of our own lives. ✣

The one thing required of the man in charge is that he be faithful to his master. Now, I am not at all concerned about being judged by you, or by any human standard; I don't even pass judgment on myself.

———

I have just made an astounding discovery! At least it is astounding for me. I have discovered that the word *success* is not in the Bible. In all sixty-six books of the Old and New Testaments the word never once appears.

It is not as though the Jews and the Greeks weren't conscious of gaining wealth or status; it is just that when they came to writing the Bible they forgot to mention success. Paul and others were concerned rather about being found faithful, trustworthy.

My discovery flies in the face of all we have been taught to believe: "the American way" and success are synonymous. Even in religion, successful churches are measured by size and income, as in a business.

Yet the Word runs counter to all this. We are judged not on the basis of our accomplishments, but by our faithfulness. Like Paul, we can be free of other people's judgments, and even of our own.

I hope that my epitaph might mention being "faithful."

The World is too much with us: late and soon,
Getting and spending, we lay waste our powers:
Little we see in Nature that is ours;
We have given our hearts away, a sordid boon!

I have just spent the morning arranging to have some cleaning and repairs done on a piece of property. Managing real estate is an honorable calling for some, but not for me. I'm not a do-it-yourselfer and I have to spend too much time and energy arranging for others to do it. I lay waste my powers. I give my heart away.

I can do only a few things well, fewer than I think. And I also suspect that there are fewer days left than I think in which to do them.

I want to live this day as though it were my last: too brief to hurry, too important to spend it in idle chatter, and too precious not to give it away.

Death is traveling without a destination,
existing without purpose,
spinning in circles,
killing time.

Death is dying without knowing
who we are,
whose we are,
why we were.

Thou madest us for Thyself, and our heart is restless until it repose in Thee.

————

Sometimes I think I know what Augustine meant about restlessness. In myself and in all around me I see discontent, aimlessness, and movement.

Do I keep moving because I am afraid to discover who I am? Do I fear death because, dead, I can no longer run and hide?

When I try hardest to put my mind at rest, I am most restless. I have tried the old escapes and the new psychology, but I am still without peace.

I ask, "Who am I?" A still, small voice whispers, "You have been created for Me and you are Mine." Not convinced, I go on living as if the whole thing were simply chance. And the anxiety hangs around like fog over the bay.

I seek a love that will not let me go, forgetting that there is no love without a Lover. Still I reject him, afraid of giving up my autonomy, my desire to do things my way.

Slowly, I become aware that my restlessness is a sign that God has not rejected me. Only when I accept his love and finally say, "Not my will, but your will," do I experience rest. ❧

And this is eternal life, that they know thee the only true God, and Jesus Christ whom thou hast sent.

Jesus came to bring us the kingdom of God, not the kingdom of endless weekends in Las Vegas. Otherwise, eternal life would be a continuous blackjack game with only fifty-two possible cards. God alone gives eternal life variety and excitement.

Yet we who spend little time exploring a relationship with God today, long for one which lasts forever. What in the name of heaven are we going to do with all of that time? We are like a youth who never calls on his girl friend before they get married.

Most of us are more curious about whether we will live after we die than we are about God. If someone died, then returned to this life and wrote a book about the experience, there would be little difficulty getting it published. And with decent design and reasonable promotion it would probably make the best-seller list in a few weeks. No matter how well written, a book on the nature of God would have a much tougher time, if indeed it could even find a publisher. God is simply not as exciting as what he can do for us.

We seem to want more life, but not more God. We are like children who snatch a gift, mumble thanks, and then become too occupied with it to notice the giver. ✒

High rollers are asked to empty their pockets,
And bet flat out that Jesus Christ lives.
Anything less or anything else
Mocks the Dealer.

Our God is a God of Salvation;
   and to God, the Lord, belongs escape from death.

———

Why do I fear death? Partly it is the fear of the unknown. Death is a journey from which no one has returned, much less given a report. Also, my senses tell me that death is a one-way trip.

Some of us may fear punishment if there is a hereafter, but more likely it is the thought of nonexistence that bothers us. It is that final separation from all we have worked for, all that we have built up, all that is near and dear to us. Our minds simply can not handle the thought of our nonexistence. What will happen to us and to everything we have personally struggled to achieve?

This final separation, this impassable gulf that separates us from all we know and love, this state of nonexistence, must be faced before the resurrection can have any possible meaning. The resurrection is not more time or extra innings but a new life, a re-creation of all that we are and know.

This is why it is impossible to earn heaven or do anything to bring it about. The resurrection is entirely up to God—upon whom we have absolutely no claims.

It is not death, but the *fear* of death that torments me; it is not dying, but the reluctance to trust God that undoes me. ❧

You shall love the Lord your God with all your heart, and with all your soul, and with all your mind.

The truth is that I do not really love God, at least not for his own sake. Rather, I love the people and things he has created. I am more interested in continuing after death a relationship with my family and friends than a relationship with God.

A priest friend said that it is easier to love a puppy than it is to love God.

I cannot pretend to love God. I can only confess my inability to do so. I can love God only as he gives me the grace to do so. Then perhaps I can also love him despite death, or, by some amazing grace, even because of it.

For death, whether of our pride or of our bodies, may yet teach us how to love God for his own sake. ❧

Why is it that some people have a simple, almost child-like (some would say "childish") faith in God's providence? They believe that they "cannot drift beyond his love or care."

Is faith a gift, like musical or athletic talent? Perhaps so, but then is there nothing we can do to acquire the gift? Or is it just given to a select few?

Faith is more like falling in love. We cannot earn the love of another person, but we can nurture the love between us. Love grows as we share ourselves, our joys and fears and desires.

Love flourishes where lovers are willing to risk. Love is a gamble; we may be misunderstood, betrayed, deserted. Love continually flies in the face of uncertainty and doubt. What lover can be certain of the everlasting love of the beloved?

If God is the supreme Lover, then it just may require a supreme risk to accept his love.

I do not have enough faith *not* to believe in God. It takes more courage than I have to conclude that life is meaningless and the grave is the end. Some people can face this abyss and still go on living useful, even joyful lives. They simply have more faith than I do.

I suppose that Christianity is a crutch for me, a crutch that enables me to walk.

I have plenty of doubts, but these are not the same as a loss of faith. Faith is trusting that God has a purpose for creating the world, even a purpose for my life. The more I realize how insignificant one life is among a billion, to say nothing about measuring it against the universe, the more amazed I am that God cares about me. Believing this is either the grossest form of egotism or the most significant fact of my existence.

Faith is a gift of God. Why he seemingly gives it to some and not to others, I do not know. All I know is that, despite the despair and hopelessness of much of life, there is a strong *yes* which I cannot shake. ❧

Why is it that I am interested
in eternity
when I have such difficulty
waiting on God?

I am angry at God for making
life so short,
I who let hours and days slip
through my fingers.

If I could only be certain that God would be with me in death, perhaps I could accept death. Yet, I know that he has been with me in life, sometimes hidden, but always present. I have felt his arms under me in the hospital, I have known his gracious touch as he has given me countless new chances, I have felt his mercy when I stubbornly refused to consider anything but my own desire.

God is the constant friend who bears with all my fits and starts, all my blindness and malice. No matter how hard I try to shake him loose, he holds fast. He is the Hound of Heaven whose "unperturbèd pace" follows me wherever I run or try to hide.

Dare I hope, though not assume, that God, who will not let me go in life, will continue to hold me fast in death?

> Nevertheless I am continually with thee;
> . . . .
> Thou dost guide me with thy counsel,
>   and afterward thou wilt receive me to glory.
> Whom have I in heaven but thee?
>   And there is nothing upon earth that I desire
>   besides thee.
> My flesh and my heart may fail,
>   but God is the strength of my heart
>   and my portion forever.

But each has his own special gift from God, one of one kind and one of another.

———

There is something ungrateful about the way I've thought about this one life God has given me. I am at the prime of life, albeit with a few creaks and squeaks, and yet I keep wondering if God does not have something better in store for me. I'm like the child who minimizes a gift, saying, "I want a better one."

Yet I can live only one life at a time. And I would like to live this life so well that if there is no other, neither God nor I will have any complaints. ❧

When we give a gift to
  someone
And see her
  cherish it
  share it
  revere it
We know how God feels when
  we love life.

A prominent San Francisco daily featured a front-page story on prostitution. The lead sentence began: "The properly established, elegantly snobbish hookers who once had this town's better streets pretty much to themselves . . ."

The article goes on to portray them as glamorous women who "would look right on a diplomat's arm." But is it not more accurate to say that they are people who have killed their feelings in order to keep their bodies alive? And what about the lack of feeling on the part of the "diplomats" who use them for an hour or so?

I do not like to think about how I prostitute myself by saying what I think people *want* to hear rather than speaking the truth in love. Could it be that I have already compromised the teachings of Jesus so much that I no longer recognize the truth? Am I a "religious hooker"?

Lord, take away our loveless death and give us your deathless love.

We cannot willingly destroy what we prize most. Before any nation can go to war, it is necessary to devalue all human life. Our own soldiers must become "dogfaces" or "grunts," the enemy "Japs" or "gooks." It is also necessary to invent myths about how cheap life is to the other side.

It would be difficult to build enthusiasm for war if we believed that something in us dies when we kill another human being. Peace could come if we loved ourselves well enough to love our sisters and brothers.

> The more I appreciate my life,
> the more I honor yours. 🍂

The dying must suffer not only
        the approach of death,
    but the withdrawal of friends fearing
        their own mortality.
Death makes bigots of us all.

What life have you, if you have not life together? There
is no life that is not in community, and no community not
lived in the praise of God.

———

My chief regret is that we may have so little time left to
be together. It is easy to be with you. I never have to
guard what I say. Even when I hurt you, you sense that I
first hurt inside.

The bond of love and friendship between us has reached
an eternal dimension: there literally is nothing on earth
that can destroy it. Søren Kierkegaard called the pact of
love "eternity's beginning in time."

Since our relationship is ultimately not dependent upon
health or wealth or the weather or moods, I would like to
think that it is not dependent upon life or death either.
Except for memories that endure for a time, however, there
really is no logical reason to assume that death does not
end a relationship.

Death is "natural" and life after death is "unnatural," or
at least not something we have a right to expect. As en-
during as our friendship is, I cannot argue from this that
it is endless. Everything else we know changes and de-
cays. Except God.

We do not talk much about God when we are together,
but we share a similar faith, a faith which sometimes enables us to talk without words.

I do not know what heaven is, so I do not know if we
will recognize each other or not. But if we are recognized
by God, then will not our friendship still be alive? ❧

We had a great weekend together. Still the sadness was always there, like a cloud bank passing in front of the sun. We appreciated it when the sun broke through, but do not the clouds also have a place?

You did not want to talk about what made us sad and that was OK. We tried to avoid speaking about it, but our careful avoidance only seemed to shout it out. Death was conspicuous by its absence in our conversation.

Afterwards I asked myself if you really did not want to talk about death or were you only trying to spare me. I wish that I had simply asked you.

Maybe we are even more afraid of sharing our feelings than we are of death. ❧

For a friend with a critical illness:

> Thank God there are no
> unforgivable sins,
> because mine would be
> leisurely writing
> about what you battle
> hand to hand. ❧

How can we be sure that death
    hasn't the last word?
It's human to try to salvage
    something from nothing,
to pretend that things aren't
    what they seem to be.
The only way that death
    doesn't defeat us
Is when life is God's
    and not ours
We keep
    only what is given back.

Think of the polite lying we do. Someone asks us: "How are you?" We give them the expected ritualistic answer: "Fine, how are you?"

Fine. Everyone is just fine. But most people are probably like me: sometimes fine, but often struggling, usually worried. I cannot "dump" on everyone, nor could I take their unloading on me, but can we not, at least sometimes, unmask a little with each other?

As I learn to die, perhaps I can learn how to share burdens with others. It is necessary to wear a mask sometimes, but I want to be able to take it off with those I care most about.

Death stands in the wings of my masquerade party. I did not invite him and I cannot make him leave. Should I ask him in, introduce him around? Maybe he is not as strange as he looks. Anyway, he is not leaving without taking us all with him.

Is death the only one who is not wearing a mask? He does not pretend to be something he is not; it is the rest of us who play games. Taxes and death are inevitable, but we can cheat only the former. ❧

We are afflicted in every way, but not crushed; perplexed, but not driven to despair; persecuted, but not forsaken; . . . always carrying in the body the death of Jesus, so that the life of Jesus may also be manifested in our bodies.

———

Intellectually I know that I am going to die, but emotionally I do not accept it. I keep thinking that something will intervene before my turn comes, like the cavalry charging up in the last reel of a western movie.

It is important that emotionally I accept my death, so that I can get on with living. As long as I think that somehow I will be the exception, I deny my humanity. When I accept death, I join the rest of the mortals.

Let me live as a dying man with compassion for my dying brothers and sisters. ✄

> Will I know that I'm free
> of death's fear
> when I'm willing to stand
> with the oppressed?

Frankly I am not certain whether I buy these words of mine or not.

The acceptance of my death has a way of making me hold even more tightly to my status and possessions. By holding onto them I preserve the illusion of immortality as long as I can.

On the other hand, I know that none of these things last. Intellectually I am prepared to let go. But would I really give away everything and work for subsistence pay? I doubt it. I would rationalize that I can be more effective where I am, holding what I have.

But freedom from the *fear* of death may yet cause me to take some risks I have been unwilling to take. Can I accept my death without it making a difference in my life?⚓

somethings are
very strange
like other
kindse of
Peaple.

I like you too.

If our sisters or brothers
were hungry or naked,
sick or in prison,
we'd rush to their aid.

But when they live in a
different part of town,
or are a different color,
we seldom see them.

Still, we fill every need,
fight every injustice
that affects *us*.

We gain, but somehow lose.

We have more than we need—
except of inner peace
and quiet conscience.

Lord, what does it mean to die
in order to live?

> Even though I walk through the valley
> of the shadow of death,
> I will fear no evil;
> for thou art with me;
> thy rod and thy staff,
> they comfort me.

God is present in his way and on his terms, not mine.

Some people claim it is God's business to love us when we are unlovable, but I doubt that. There is no more reason for him to love us than for me to love a disloyal friend.

All my life I have related to God on a commercial basis: What have you done for me lately, Lord? Even when I think that I am "serving" him, I am really serving myself: when I preach a sermon, I want people to thank me. When I write a book about faith, I want the tangible results of a readership. When I help someone, I expect gratitude.

Never would I hold on to a friend who treated me in the shabby way I treat God. Yet even when I use and abuse God, he is ready with his rod and his staff to comfort me. Despite all my rebellion and disobedience, he remains steadfast. Despite all I do to kill our relationship, he is always present with me.

God is present in his way, not mine. He does not remove the valley of the shadow; he stays with me in it. In doubt and fear I go to the hospital to comfort a dying person, only to discover that through the patient God comforts me. ❧

I tell you, my friends, do not fear those who kill the body, and after that have no more that they can do.

We have focused so much on physical death that we have forgotten that real death is the death of the human spirit.

There are people on skid row whose spirits are dead while their bodies live on. But what about the business executive who "has everything" except hope and joy? What about the preacher who preaches the good news without feeling good inside? What about the best-selling author who feels he has written drivel?

Why can we not get as excited about the cure for the cancer of our spirits as we are about a cure for the cancer of our bodies?

I cannot possibly understand why a serious illness strikes a good person in the prime of life—someone with a dependent family, someone at the height of a promising career, someone near and dear. It is a dark and awful mystery. The classic attempts to explain tragedy and rationalize evil only mock the question.

The only glimmer of light that makes sense to me is that maybe God himself is still struggling to overcome evil. Maybe he does not have it all made. Maybe God's battle is still going on, not only against disease, but against everything that attacks our bodies and spirits.

Some people may consider it blasphemous to suggest that God does not have unlimited power. But if he could cure every cancer, why does he not do so? I prefer to believe that God has created a world in which he does not have total power. I would rather believe that than to believe that he is callous and indifferent to our suffering.

Meanwhile, in the midst of death all we can do is to affirm life, believing that we are not alone in our struggle. ❧

If thou, O Lord, shouldst mark iniquities,
    Lord, who could stand?
But there is forgiveness with thee,
    that thou mayest be feared.

I toss and turn in the middle of the night thinking of some stupid thing I said, or some person I hurt, or some situation I blew. What if hell is a continuous videotape of these things played back in living color? No wonder I have eliminated hell from my theology! Or have I?

I have not been able to eliminate the ability to feel regret. This feeling is often appropriate, but what do I do with it? It can hang around me like the life-killing smog in Los Angeles. Unrelieved regret can kill the spirit and even help to kill the body. Something has to give. Somehow there must be a resurrection from the death of the past, a release from remorse, before a resurrection of the body means anything. Who wants to be resurrected to an eternity of regret? Far better to sleep in the grave forever.

The story of Jesus is about God taking my selfishness, my betrayals, my callousness upon himself. If God does that, he speaks directly to my regrets. Not only are my sins forgiven, but they are forgiven by the One who knows me best, or rather worst. There is nothing I have done, can do, or will do, that God is not aware of and willing to set aside, to cancel forever. God alone has a mind big enough to forget my sin.

I am relieved that everything about me is known by none except God. And I find it incredible that he who, knowing me best, should be most offended, is most willing to forgive. ❦

Do we want to live forever—
    and weather like Old Baldy or Half Dome?
Even they will someday crumble
    and turn to dust.
        Live forever when marathon races end,
    as do presidential terms, thank God.

Worse than death
    is running in place
        forever.

For we do not know how to pray as we ought, but the
Spirit himself intercedes for us with sighs too deep for
words.

———

I groan a lot. Groaning, they say, can be a form of
prayer.

My constant groan is: "God help me." But I am not
sure what I mean by those words.

Would I like God to solve my problems for me? Frankly,
yes. Even though most of them have been of my own
making, I am not keen on suffering in order to build
character.

If I had a terminal illness, would I like God to heal me?
Most assuredly.

But would I really want God to abolish death? Do I
really want to go on living forever on this earth? Some
people think there is a possibility of that in the future. I
want to live long enough to do a few things well. But
when I soberly consider the possibility of being Bob Herhold forever, I am not excited. This life seems designed
for brevity.

When I groan, I hope I am pleading for more than an
extension of time. I hope that I am interested in discover-
ing and fulfilling the purpose for which I have been given
life. ❧

My father died from a blood disease after receiving over two hundred transfusions. He was kept alive by transfusions, intravenous feedings, and drugs. While his body declined, his spirit grew. Once, after receiving the Eucharist from his pastor, he said: "My soul is clean. The sheets are clean. Why can't I go?"

> Some people find it possible
> to surrender freely.
> They are not more courageous,
> only more experienced. ✣

For a day in thy courts is better
than a thousand elsewhere.
. . . .
For a thousand years in thy sight
are but as yesterday when it is past,
or as a watch in the night.

———

It is impossible to tell time as God tells time. Our minds cannot jump in and out of their accustomed time frames without experiencing a cosmic jet lag.

Still, to know that "a thousand years . . . are but as yesterday" gives a different dimension to life. We grieve when a young person dies; later there may be some comfort in considering that life is measured in more than years.

I believe that today can be "a day in thy courts" and "better than a thousand elsewhere." Yet each day is like a broken record. I keep repeating the same old mistakes, demonstrating the same old weaknesses. I wonder if I will ever change. Will I ever get out of this rut?

Then I am jarred by the sudden news of another's serious illness. There is no marked change in my life, except that I realize now, as I never realized before, that the future is now. The day when I am going to study my priorities, set aside petty concerns, and become a mature and loving person is today. There is no more time; there are no more chances.

Since I am given only one day at a time, and no guarantee that I will live until tomorrow, I have a new freedom. I am free from having to regret all the time I wasted in the past, since no thing or no sin need contaminate the present. Therefore, today can be better than all my yesterdays. I do not have to wait for future joy; I can have it today. ✒

Surely goodness and mercy shall follow me
all the days of my life;
and I shall dwell in the house of the Lord
for ever.

———

The amazing experiences of God's care each day lead me to believe that he does not give up caring after I die. There is no logical reason, however, why this should be so. But then there is no logical reason, either, why he should care for me each day.

Floating on a cloud or walking on gold streets holds little allure for me. Nor does a continuous Sunday School picnic—I have been on enough of those annual outings to know that if they exist in the hereafter, heaven will not be the place for them. And I can't imagine holding a harp, when I never even listen to one now, much less play one.

There is no picture of heaven that turns me on nearly as much as what I am doing here and now. With all of its frustrations and pain, I still prefer this life to any unknown heaven. When the Lord calls, please tell him I am busy.

Still, I wonder why the Creator made us and what possible future he has in mind. I am more than idly curious about what kind of a Mind conceived all this and why. Even more, what kind of a Heart would endure our aeons of rebuff and still love us?

I want to stay here as long as possible, but I also feel a strange tug from the future. ✖

Naked from his mother's womb he came, as naked as he came he will depart again; nothing to take with him after all his efforts.

———

Why should we arrogant little creatures who kill each other and tear up the good earth expect to be given another place? That would be like rewarding a kid with a Porsche after he's totaled your Volkswagen.

What right have we to assume that God owes us anything after this life? We came into the world naked, and we leave the world naked. In the name of what kind of justice can we claim more?

Maybe people who do not believe in life after death are more religious than those of us who feel that we have a post-mortem lien on God. If they think of God, it is not as the guarantor of their immortality. Others of us sometimes think that God exists only to put our name in lights on a heavenly marquee.

Jesus talked about our entering into the kingdom of God. He did not talk about our personal forty-watt bulbs burning forever by themselves. In the kingdom we will know what it means to worship God for his own sake, and not simply for what he gives us. ✄

Before him will be gathered all the nations.

———

The loneliness of death is what I dread most. I like being alone for brief periods of time, but I hate long spans of loneliness. I find my life in relationship with other people.

Some people think we have a divine spark in us that never goes out, like a forever-ready battery. I hope that we do not, because if we did, it might be my luck to have my spark sparkling off on some remote galaxy, a thousand light years from everyone else's.

I am glad Jesus did not talk about individual immortality, but about the kingdom of God. ❧

The free gift of God is eternal life in Christ Jesus our Lord.

———

There is something about God's love and providence that makes me feel that this life leads to something. I have been steered through too many mine fields for me to believe that it all ends with a cosmic bang or a human whimper. But if our personhood lives after death, it is only because God values persons.

The best way that I can fend off an egocentric idea of heaven is to realize that whatever heaven is, it surely is not more of the same. It is not my ego striving against other egos, or my book competing for a place on a celestial shelf, or my addressing a larger congregation than the preacher on a neighboring cloud. It is not pleasing myself or "doing my thing" through all eternity. That would surely be hell, not heaven.

Heaven by definition is radically different from what we have known. Yet there are intimations in the here and now. Occasionally, by grace, I do something for someone without wholly seeking my own benefit, and in so doing I experience a little rapture. Sometimes, with more grace, I comfort someone, and in so doing I experience much comfort. And, with a massive infusion of grace, I sometimes want to please God as much as I do myself, and then for a moment I know an unspeakable joy.

I want to love and serve God *without* the carrot of heaven. The future is in his hands alone. ❧

Simon, Simon, behold, Satan demanded to have you, that
he might sift you like wheat, but I have prayed for you.

Katherine Hepburn was once asked by an interviewer if
she ever wished she had had children. She said no and
explained that she could not have been both an actress and
a mother. She also did not think that she would have
made a very good mother.

"You cannot have it all," she said. "You simply cannot
have it all. Some people feel that they can have two or
three roles, but I found long ago that acting took everything
I have."

Hepburn's conclusions run counter to much of American
folklore. The athletic heroes in high school and college
are the three- and four-letter people. Versatility, rather
than specialization, is praised. It is popular to talk about
people having several careers in a lifetime. Some people
say that this is ideal.

I have tried to do many things, sometimes simultane-
ously. Slowly and painfully I am coming to realize that if
I can be a husband and father, minister to a small congregation, and write a few pieces, I will be fortunate and
happy. I cannot be all things; perhaps I can be a few
things. When Jesus said: "Happy are the pure in heart;
they will see God!" he had in mind not cleanliness of
thought, but simplicity of purpose. ❧

We struggle for our first
   and last breaths
In order to perfect the moment
   in between.

I've made a virtue of being
      broad,
      wide-ranging,
      tolerant.

Now I'd like to be
      channeled,
      sharpened,
      surgical.

I'm more interested in a fine carving
      than in sawing a forest.

> Take from our souls the strain and stress,
> And let our ordered lives confess
> The beauty of thy peace.

———

I have always been past- or future-oriented. Either I spend my energy regretting the sins and mistakes of the past or I dream about a nonexistent future. It is a wonder I get anything done in the present.

I am beginning to take the ticking of the clock seriously. And instead of panicking because I have so little time left, I am experiencing a small but growing sense of order and serenity in each day.

When I sort out priorities and begin to live by them, I feel much better about myself. I am also starting to discover the joy of doing a few things well.

But I still need a rein on my ambitions. They run so wide that only death sets bounds which I am forced to recognize. My death reminds me that I have only a limited time to do a few things reasonably well.

It is God's way of saying to me: "You can't have it all."

Take heed, watch; for you do not know when the time will come.

A close friend has been told that he has a terminal illness. He has seen his lawyer and has gotten his affairs in order.

What does it mean to get one's affairs in order? Certainly there is the matter of a will and estate planning. And maybe discussion of final arrangements and funeral.

But there is a sense in which we can never have our affairs in order. Our life is always in a state of becoming or else we would have completed all our tasks.

If our lives have been created for God, then we will always be growing toward him. A sign of our progress in that direction is an awareness of how far we still have to go. As with outer space, the more we discover, the more there is left to discover.

Perhaps it is best that we die traveling on an unlimited journey.

So teach us to number our days
  that we may get a heart of wisdom.

———

I once saw a young man in a Boston cemetery making an imprint from a tombstone by rubbing a crayon against the back of a piece of tracing paper. I paid him to make one for me which read:

Here lies Buried

the Body of

Cap. John Decoster

who died Jan^{Y} 28th

1773. Aged 26. Years.

Stop here my Friend & Cast an Eye
As you are now so Once was i
As i am now so you must be
Prepare for Death & Follow me.

It hangs on the back of my study door, but I seldom read it as I rush in and out. One would think that I might at least glance at it now and then.

Just to keep myself honest. ❦

> In our sleep, pain which cannot forget falls drop by drop upon the heart until, in our own despair, against our will, comes wisdom through the awful grace of God.

———

Robert Kennedy quoted this passage from Aeschylus right after he heard the news of Martin Luther King's assassination. The next day he spoke of violence to the City Club of Cleveland: "Our lives on this planet are too short, and the work to be done too great, to let this spirit flourish any longer in our land."

I just watched a rerun of "All in the Family." Four adults shouted at each other constantly for twenty-seven minutes. My uneasiness betrays the fact that I can be as unreasonable as Archie and as quarrelsome as Mike. I protest physical violence, yet I practice psychological violence. When will I ever realize that life is as short as . . . as a television program? Only there are no reruns.

Death may sober us, even teach us how to live each today better than yesterday. But as soon as we acquire some skills, death blows his whistle.

Life, not death, is sweet. The only sweetness in death is what it teaches us about life. But why is it that we so quickly forget what death is trying to teach us?

That forgetting, rather than death itself, may be the real tragedy. ❧

Death be not proud, though some have called thee
Mighty and dreadful, for, thou art not so.

―――

Death has a very bad press. Yet aren't there some good words we can say for it?

Surely it is merciful to those who lie suffering from an incurable illness. When the machines we have developed will not let death complete its mission of mercy, can we call that progress?

Death is often a welcome visitor for those who have lived active lives and now wait with waned and enfeebled powers. Death is a friend to some who have outlived friends and family, and long to join their rest.

The footsteps of death can be wisdom for the strong and youthful. Each footfall says that death is waiting for us and that life must be embraced at this moment. ⌘

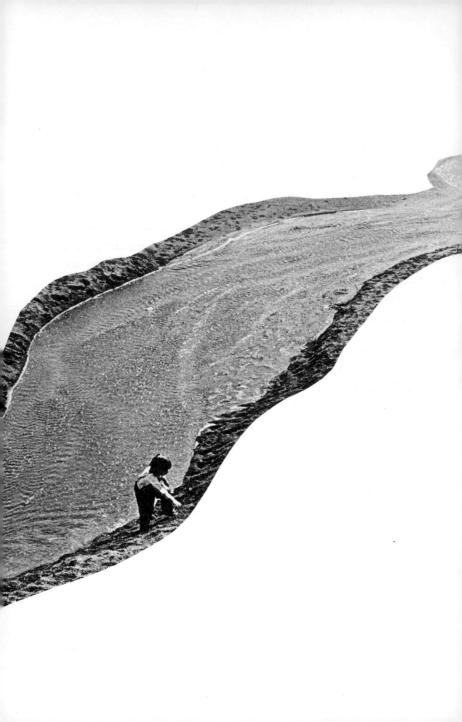

Death sets boundaries like
    the banks of a river.
Otherwise our lives would
    be ankle-deep lakes.
Power comes not from a flood,
    but from a stream.

. . . and with his stripes we are healed.

How did it go with you, Jesus, when you died? Did you go through all of the stages of dying? Did you deny death, feel isolated, become angry, bargain with God, feel depressed, and finally accept it?

How did you feel, Jesus, when your disciples understood nothing of what you were about? Did you feel that they would never get the message and that you had wasted your life?

When the sweat came like "great drops of blood" were you shaking your fist at your Father? Worse yet, did you feel like you were talking to the wind, Jesus?

When you prayed, "Let this cup pass from me," did you promise your Father what you would do if only you could go on living? Did you explain how confused and weak your followers were and that you planned to spend more time with them if only you were granted an extension?

Did your anger turn to despair, Jesus, when you saw your friends flee? How did you feel when one betrayed you for money and another openly said that he had never known you?

Were you frightened, Jesus, when you heard the clank of armor and saw your friend leading the authorities to arrest you? Did your knees buckle when the band of soldiers seized you? Did your voice tremble before Herod and Pilate? Did you shake all night in prison? Did you choke into speechlessness when they lowered the cross on your back? Did you think you would never get up when you stumbled on the way to your execution? What kinds of stares did you get from the curious onlookers along that narrow street?

Did you feel confident God was with you as they drove the nails into your hands and feet, or did you feel only pain? Did you feel like a fool when they hoisted the cross into place and the soldiers jeered? Did you wish, for an instant, that you could get even with them for torturing you all night?

How did you feel when the holy men jeered that you had saved others but could not save yourself? Did you have the sinking feeling that maybe they were right?

What was it like to have given yourself totally to God's cause only to have him abandon you at the end? Did you have the terrible thought that your Father was maybe like Judas? When you died placing yourself into his hands, were you afraid that he might not catch you?

Jesus, if thoughts like these entered your head, then you know all about *my* fear of dying. I am grateful that my death could not possibly be worse than yours. I am also grateful that I have not been tested like you were. I hope I never will be.

Should the unthinkable happen, stay with me, Jesus. Maybe thinking about you will help. But if I knew that you were thinking about me, that would help even more. ❧

Jesus, knowing that the Father had given all things into his hands, and that he had come from God and was going to God, rose from supper, laid aside his garments, and girded himself with a towel. Then he poured water into a basin, and began to wash the disciples' feet.

———

Jesus, I think I know what made you what you were. John's little aside about coming from God and going to God tells it all. You were able to strip yourself of your privilege as well as your clothes, take a towel and a basin, and go to work as a servant. It was because you knew who you were and where you were going that you were able to spend yourself totally. You demonstrated the connection between accepting one's destiny and fulfilling it here on earth.

But yours is a most difficult act to follow. If I fully accepted the idea that I came from God and am going to God, it would make drastic changes in my lifestyle. I am afraid to ask what taking up a towel means for me. Does it mean lowering my standard of living so that others can live? Does it mean leaving my comfortable study and going to the city jail to visit people? Does it mean asking how they got there?

I am not sure that I want to strip myself of all that I have and start washing feet, even figuratively.

Jesus, must all of me die
before I can live? ❧

We must keep on doing the works of him who sent me, as long as it is day; the night is coming, when no one can work.

Jesus, how did you accomplish so much in three years? Was it because you had a premonition of your death? Did you avoid trivial words because you knew you had only so many words allotted to you? Did you know that you would not have a second opportunity with many people?

Jesus, did you worry about leaving a monument? I worry a lot about accomplishing something in the brief time I have. In fact, I sometimes panic. I even think that maybe *you* are counting on me to do something. Did thoughts about your own accomplishments also enter your mind, Jesus?

Is it wrong to be ambitious, Jesus? Is it wrong to want to leave more of a mark than a fist leaves when removed from a bucket of water? Were not your disciples and Paul ambitious? Was their sole motivation to make you known? Did not they too have egos?

Help me to have the kind of ambition that will serve your purposes, Jesus.

Today, before the night comes. ❧

74

Is death when the heart stops beating
or when it stops loving?

Death is teaching me to appreciate a few close people while I can. I have had good friends die before I told them how much they meant to me. Not any longer. I want to tell people *now* how much I love them, not in a eulogy. I want to clasp them to me tightly, so they will know of my love.

I wonder if my wife knows how much I appreciate her, how grateful I am that she supports me without pandering to my weaknesses, how thankful I am that she remains a wife even when I think I need a mother.

Do my kids know how fortunate I consider myself to be their father, how much I admire their sensitivity and their desire to make a contribution? They are further along toward this goal than many people twice their age. I must tell them.

A magazine sent me a promotional piece which said I might win a prize if I returned their certificate. I returned it immediately, before the offer expired. Why am I not equally prompt in noting the thoughtfulness and mentioning the contributions of others?

Death, whatever else you may be, you are a firm reminder that I have only a short time in which to appreciate these folks—and let them know it.

Before the limited offer expires. &

This is my commandment, that you love one another as I have loved you.

———

Suicide often creates more problems than it solves, even when people think they are relieving others of burdens.

Two of my friends recently took their lives. In both cases they were deeply troubled and felt they were a burden on others. I wish I had told them otherwise. I wish I had told them how important they were to me, how much I needed their love.

God's grace is sufficient for them and also for me. There is nothing I can do for them now—except to listen to other cries of pain.

> Today we can write the letter,
> pay the visit,
> dial the call,
> buy the gift,
> share the joy.
> Today is the grace of God
> converted into time. ❧

This morning I accused my wife of mislaying a letter, and then I found it among my things.

Cannot death soften my relations with others? Instead of fighting death, can I not make him an ally? If I knew that this morning would be the last morning I would see my wife, would I not act differently?

Death and love need each other. By forcing me to realize my limited opportunities for showing affection, death increases love. By never giving up, love turns the harshness of death into hope.

When I think of the countless new chances God has given me, I am awed. A friend of mine said that if he were in charge of himself, he would have given up long ago.

The forgiveness I am going to seek, the words of understanding and hope I plan to speak, the deeds of kindness I intend to perform must be done now.

Before the night comes. ✹

Because I live, you will live also.

I fell to the ground and heard a voice.

The presence and power of God came to me during an illness a few years ago. After several operations it seemed like my bed and I were sinking through the floor into a bottomless pit of quicksand. Then a strange feeling took hold of me. It was as though my bed and I had suddenly hit bottom and the bottom held. The ground under me was solid!

I did not hear God speak, nor did I come to understand divine mysteries. But I knew that my suffering, and even my death, did not say the last word about me.

Jesus, your life had more purpose to it than any life I know. As I get close to you I can feel the fire that burned within you. With your whole life you said that you were on earth to love and to serve God. You said it as you turned away from flattery. You said it as you called weak and common people to your side, trusting the Spirit to make them strong and uncommon. You said it as you rejected our kingdom in favor of your Father's, and as you chose God's will over your own— even in the face of death.

Jesus, I worry about life after death, but am involved in death after birth. I court people's favorable opinion while neglecting to consider yours. If life after death is more of my unrelenting self-centeredness, then everlasting sleep is preferable. But if eternal life is having your mind and your spirit, let this gift be mine—today!

Jesus, help me to discover eternal life before I die. ✄

Whether we live or whether we die, we are the Lord's.

There is no peace with life until we have made peace with death. But "peace with death" is more than a stoic acknowledgment of death. To say that we are all going to die and that there is nothing we can do about it, is not *peace* with death.

Peace with death is a profound awareness that *I*—not just mankind—am going to die. Someday *my* heart will beat no more, *my* lips will speak no words, *my* eyes will see no beauty, and *I* will cease to exist by any and all measurements. The next thing will be for my family, through the means of someone who "undertakes" the job, to dispose of my body in as efficient a way as possible.

Yet, is there not a contradiction in saying that a living person must accept the fact that he or she is going to die? Does not such an admission contradict the "will to live" which is necessary if we are to continue living?

The will to live is an affirmation of life which means, among other things, taking care of my body and mind. It does not mean denying the obvious fact that I am going to die; that would not be the will to live, but the will to live an illusion.

Peace with death and the will to live are really brothers. When I acknowledge without fear or complaint that I am going to die, then I am free to live.

Brave talk—except that the source of such courage is the faith that "whether we live or whether we die, we are the Lord's." That we go to heaven after we die is not so important. What matters is that God is with us in death, as he is with us in life. That life and death are "both alike to thee." ❧

For I am sure that neither death,
nor life,
nor angels,
nor principalities,
nor things present,
nor things to come,
nor powers,
nor height,
nor depth,
nor anything else in all creation,
will be able to separate us from the love of God
in Christ Jesus our Lord.

A CLOSE FRIEND recently began a challenging and creative job. Shortly afterwards he was hospitalized with a serious disease and shared some of his thoughts:

I'm playing it (death) as though it isn't going to happen. My drive comes from the belief that my potential exceeds my accomplishments and I just need time to bring the two even a little closer together. If time is running out—I'm wiped out. So in truth I haven't accepted the fact and therefore it's painful to talk about it.

Later he reflected further:

I felt that any contemplation of death was counter-productive. I'm still struggling with it, but it no longer seems a major contradiction to set goals and have a commitment to the future and at the same time accept the inevitability of death, whenever it may come. Better to die doing a job I like than waiting in an armchair.

He is an athletic, active person who found a hospital isolation room difficult:

One of the hellish things about being in isolation is the endless time to contemplate in silence. . . . It's not only the loneliness . . . I find that contemplating death is a bore and a real drag. . . . Maybe loneliness is God's way of bringing us closer to him. No one else really understands.

With his indomitable spirit, he soon went back to work. However, his illness still hovers overhead like a cloud:

The thing I dread most is that people may treat me differently because I may have a terminal illness. That would really kill me! God spare me from the sympathy of others. I'm the same person, with the same strengths and weaknesses. I want people to get mad at me when I do stupid things, as well as praise me for those occasional good things I do. . . . In short, any change in other people's relationship to me, based upon sympathy, would in itself be an untimely death.

He concluded by saying:

The other feeling I have is one of complete frustration—somewhat like playing a losing football game. (I'm well qualified.) Every play offers some hope, but it's increasingly hard to get psyched up. Finally, you know that even the long bomb won't pull it out. You mechanically play it out, but frustration ends in despair and the end of the game comes as a blessing.

My friend and I have grown closer than ever during his illness. He does not wear his religion like a school emblem on a sports coat, nor has he suddenly become interested in God. Rather, his faith has been a quiet reserve upon which he frequently has drawn. The possibility of an untimely death comes as a shock, but not as a shock which will crumble or destroy him.

I find it as hard to accept the possibility of his death as he does. He is one of those friends who appear only once in a lifetime. Each of us knows instinctively where the other is at, and we often communicate as much by our silences as we do by our sounds. When I leave him I never have the feeling that something either of us said may

have been misunderstood. We understand each other even when our thoughts come out half-baked. We are each other's best audience and laugh with abandon at each other's worst jokes. We have been friends all our lives. He has even forgiven me for conning him into taking a fourteen-mile Boy Scout hike with me when he was only eight.

I am the one who cannot let go. I do not expect to find another friend like him. I am grateful that I have shared some of his life and I hope to share more of it. I am puzzled and angry that our friendship may end.

Lord, is there some way that you will not let our friendship die even though we die? ✻

My CHIEF qualification for doing this little book is the same as every reader's: I am dying. I do not have a particular disease nor has the doctor cautioned me, but I am dying. The only difference between the healthiest of us and the sickest of us is a matter of time. We begin to die the day we are born.

I have not yet come to grips with my own death. I never shall fully. But I would like to be instructed by death. This is all I can hope for, because being alive means constantly resisting death. But I want to resist it without denying its reality or missing what it has to teach me.

Martin Luther King had a premonition of death on the night before he was killed. He spoke of having been "to the mountain top," suggesting that his work might be finished. He said "longevity has its place," but declared that he was ready to die if necessary. He accepted his own death without seeking it. He had both the willingness to die and the desire to live. This is what I seek.

I suppose I have another qualification that is less universal: I once underwent five operations, with all possible complications except death. I was sure I was dying and wrote separate notes to my wife and to each of my children. I said to one of them that I had "absolutely no fear." In part I was whistling to keep up my courage, but I also felt so sick that my hold on life was not strong. Finally, and most significantly, I had a sense of God as the Ground under me. I can only hope that I might fare as well in the real encounter with death as I did in the dress rehearsal.

While I may not so much fear the actual moment of death, I loathe the thought of going through the dying process again. I do not want to fade slowly away mentally and physically; I would prefer that the light burn brightly until the end and then go off all at once. Yet even the prospect of an uncomfortable or a lingering death does not totally shatter me; I once felt that my body was being used for medical research while I still needed it, but God was with me then and I trust he will be with me in the future.

I do not fear dying before I have completed the few things God put me on earth to accomplish. No one knows how many or how much this is, but at fifty-one I feel as though I have only started to live. My brother tells me that if I ever got it all together, I could be dangerous.

More than my own death, I fear the death of those whom I love. I fear that my children might not live to realize their potential, or that my wife might die before I do. This too is selfish since what I really fear is my being abandoned by them. I can disturb the best night's sleep with such thoughts of separation. What makes me think that God, who did not forget me, will forget them—or me in their absence?

I also fear the death of this amazing planet God has given us. The syndicated writer Art Hoppe occasionally writes a column about the Landlord and Gabriel discussing whether or not Gabriel should take up his trumpet and sound the eviction notice for the unruly and ungrateful tenants back on that "tiny little planet that keeps giving us so much trouble." Gabriel notes that "the louder they complain about conditions down there, the less they want to leave the place." The Landlord sighs: "It isn't that I made the heavens too dim; it's that I made the earth too fair." No matter what heaven may hold, I am reluctant to part with this fair earth—or to see it destroyed by us unruly and ungrateful tenants.

The fear of death is reinforced by the destruction of the body and the unknown nature of anything beyond the grave. Common sense tells us that "when you're dead, you're dead." Period. All our sensory experience denies anything beyond our rejoining the elements. How does anyone make anything out of a handful of ashes? An atheist serving as custodian at a seminary was noted for baiting the young theologians. He accosted one who was reading a book on eternal life: "If you ask me, that's so much hogwash. When you're dead, you're dead," he snorted. The student paused, smiled, and said: "You're right, George, when you're dead, you're dead." George went away scratching his head and murmuring, "What in the world is that guy doing in the seminary?"

The student commented that any hope of eternal life comes only after people have faced the reality of death, just as George did. Whatever life after death is, it is not simply a continuation of this life. Death is a radical break with life as we know it. It is not simply the death of our bodily functions, but the end of all our ties to people and things, to our plans and projects, to our hopes and dreams.

One of the reasons I fight death is that I do not want to let go of all I hold dear in this life. Why should I? All that I have has been given to me by God, and I cannot take lightly such gifts.

Yet, somehow if I can loosen my grip on these gifts and hold chiefly to the Giver, I think that I can face death with some tranquillity. The God who gives me my life is with me in death, and whatever he then does with me can only be good.

It is easy to move from a loosened grip on the world to a rejection of the world. Instead of being God's wondrous gift, the creation is seen as a "vale of tears" which we are advised to pass through as rapidly as possible. This is like sprinting through an exhibit of van Gogh paintings while wearing dark glasses.

The opposite reaction is to rush through life grabbing as much as we can, like those people on the television shows who are given grocery carts and five minutes in which to assemble as much loot as they can. "Eat, drink, and be merry for tomorrow we die" is as accepted today as it was in ancient Rome. Life is too brief not to have a little fun, and fun often means something which tends to make life even briefer. A cartoon showed a doctor examining a sagging, obese man and saying, "Wine and women are out, but you can sing all you want."

A different option, and the one to which this little book is dedicated, is that death can be a teacher. Despite all of its unfairness and untimeliness, death can instruct us. Since we can only live one life at a time, it seems reasonable to ask what death can teach us about *this* life. Any life after death is meaningless unless we have found purpose and joy in the life we *now* live.

When we let death turn us away from this life to the next one, or when we let it panic us into an orgy of pleasure, we miss death as teacher. Death becomes a teacher when we ask what we can learn from it to enhance life today.

The best kind of learning takes place when we are able to apply the lesson to an immediate problem or situation. If the chief lesson of death is that we die before entering heaven, then death may teach us about preparing for the life to come, but little about this life. If death, however, is meant primarily to teach us how to live here and now, then it has immediate application. Learning to die can mean learning to live!

It is important to note that from God's perspective there is no distinction between "this life" and "the life to come." Life with God is one life. Jesus said it succinctly: "And this is eternal life, that they know thee the only true God, and Jesus Christ whom thou has sent" (John 17:3).

For death to become my teacher I do not have to understand it, any more than I have fully understood my other teachers. I do not have to like death either; after all, I have learned significant lessons from people and from situations I did not like. Death is willing to become my teacher, not my buddy. The main requirement is that I acknowledge a need to discover how to live more fully and creatively, and be open to what death can teach me.

The reflections I have shared here on what death is teaching me about life are in no sense a finished treatise on the subject. I hope to remain under death's tutelage until I draw my last breath and, only then, graduate. ❧

I am grateful to Peter Brown, a graduate student in photography at Stanford University, for adding his artistry to this book; most of the pictures are his contribution. Additional photographs are the work of Michael Paulson (page 57), Lise Giodesen (pages 62 and 76), and Daniel David Derr (pages 71 and 80); their talents are likewise appreciated.

My thanks to Robert McAfee Brown for his helpful suggestions, to Edith Carter for her literary and secretarial skills, and to Edward A. Cooperrider of Fortress Press for his amazing editorial grace. Joseph and Jeanne Sittler have done much to increase my faith and to inform my theology.

Finally, this book was made possible because family, parishioners, and other friends continue to teach me how to die and how to live.

ROBERT M. HERHOLD

Quotations on the following pages within the book are from the sources indicated: